Heather Island

Heather Island
Joan McBreen

salmonpoetry

Published in 2009 by
Salmon Poetry
Cliffs of Moher, County Clare, Ireland
Website: www.salmonpoetry.com
Email: info@salmonpoetry.com

Paperback ISBN 978-1-907056-01-7
Hardback ISBN 978-1-907056-02-4

Cover artwork: *Moody Day, The Big House in the Distance with Dark Trees*,
2006, oil on canvas, by STUART SHILS, The Fenton Gallery, Cork
Typesetting: Siobhán Hutson

for Joseph, Max, Mia and Molly

Acknowledgements

Acknowledgements are due to the editors of the following publications where these poems, or versions of them, first appeared:

Poetry Ireland Review, Force 10, The Clifden Anthology, The Irish Times, Best of Irish Poetry 2008, The Tuam Herald, An Sionnach, Vol. 2 No. 162, Creighton University Press and *The Bend, Number One – Irish Poetry Supplement* – Notre Dame University.

Special thanks to Niall MacMonagle, Brendan Flynn, Eamon Grennan, Caroline Geraghty, Jim Carney, Geraldine Mitchell, Nuala Ní Dhomhnaill, Ernest Lyons, Joe Woods, Helen McBreen, Brian McBreen and Joe McBreen for invaluable help and encouragement.

Also special gratitude to the poets involved in my work as editor of *The Watchful Heart – A New Generation of Irish Poets – Poems and Essays.*

The author wishes to include a special thanks to Stuart Shils, the artist whose painting *Moody Day, The Big House in the Distance with Dark Trees* graces the cover of this book.

Author's royalties from this book donated to Cancer Care West, University College Hospital, Galway.

Contents

I

II

III

I

Montbretia on the High Road, Renvyle

Between hedge and house
montbretia flares.
Slow rain falls. September,
season of stillness,

of hoar-frost
and early dusk. From here
at the edge of the world
summer's birds take off

from rowans laden
with fruit. When you left
absence and distance
became companions, familiar

as the curves on the road
and Tully mountain
in the kind of light
only this landscape knows.

I will begin again
as montbretia bulbs
send out white roots
in water, on a window-sill.

Ballinakill

Roses take their battering,
the most stubborn clinging
to gables, resisting November.

Darkness gathers over
the harbour and though
you have made your way there

you are outside it. Water rises,
trees on the shore turn
towards what light is left.

I dreamed I stood at the end
of a pier, black oaks
hurled around in a storm.

Far out at sea a foghorn is heard,
disconsolate cry of the lost.

Derryinver

Bleak the browning bracken
on the road descending to the harbour.
Tully behind us, the sheep, marked orange
and blue, embroider the fields.
Late blackberries ruined by rain
rot in the ditches and the colours
on the hillside, greys and lavenders
of October, remind us we are back
where a well-built bridge is across
a river and we shape ourselves
not into twilight but into walking
upright, faster, remembering
that pictures of the past are not lost
even if the mist grows ghostly and cold.

Omey

Solitude, rain and the road,
the tide not yet turned, wide
stretches of sand behind.

Spring returns. I push my fingers
deep into the earth and steal
from Omey her first primroses.

On this island, coast of wild rocks,
sea, fields and waves come together
and hundreds of seabirds

become souls set free,
wheeling in the wind, unhurried
in a vast sky, beyond sound.

Hawthorn on the High Road

The bay trees I placed
either side of my blue door
are shrivelled by a salt wind,
and rowans on the lawn
carry and shelter linnet and thrush.

After you left, it was to bridal
hawthorn I turned,
fragile to touch yet strong
enough to endure.

I listen to the wind rise,
to the reeds on Tully Lake
whisper their story. Two swans move
towards Heather Island, elegant
with plumage of white velvet.

Heather Island

for Eamon Grennan

November sunlight shines
on Tully Lake, on the slate roof
of your house.

When the High Road was tarred
and new water pipes laid
along the field between us,

sallies and fuchsias
were dragged up by the roots.
The lake endured when dusk fell.

The song birds left
for Heather Island. Mourning
their loss, I pulled my scarf

tighter around my throat.
The sky will argue with the wind,
with the whole of bird lore

and scattered whin,
sally and fuchsia –
their sheltering branches.

II

Loss

Loss is a handkerchief on blackthorn touched with frost,
the imprint of your feet on sands you have crossed.

Loss is many stations where you waved in the rain,
the spring and summer you will not see again.

Loss is the mother calling the boy who does not reply,
is forked lightning in a summer sky.

Loss is the last page of each book loved,
is in the bedroom curtains that have not moved.

Loss is the black gabardine never returned,
it has no colour – that too is learned.

Loss is a silence you cannot forget,
is tobacco smoke recalled in the lilac garden where we met.

Daughter in July Downpour

The rain is falling hard, my dear,
from skies immense and cold,
heart-breaking and record-breaking
and I grow old, so old.

But soon it will be blackberry time,
come back in the autumn air
and with the end of summer
I will wind late flowers in your hair.

I will give you a bouquet of marguerites
and the rain will cease to matter
for the fragrance will last into the night,
in the morning white petals will scatter.

Cherry Blossom in May

I

The cherry trees in bloom
and time so short.

Petals cover the path today
where the bride in her finery
walks, her veil drenched
with pink rain.

II

The night you were born
I wished none I loved
were wakeful.

We slept, you and I,
moonlight creeping through
the window and you, my girl,
were unaware of leaves
rustling and blossoms

falling to earth.

In Memory of Louis MacNeice

There hidden by pale shrubbery
he watched his mother walk
the garden path, in tears.

Between the poems and the life
this haunted him, his childhood
road closed.

Always he heard her voice
from night shadows –
a scent of jasmine

at the gate she opened
and walked through.

Winter Light at Lissadell

Trees are the same
as in my childhood –
oaks, rowans and silver birch.
Winter light is still
shining over water,
bent grass and Knocknarea.

But the people I knew
are gone.
Purser's Constance and Eva
stare out from a canvas.
The ghosts of my parents
pick bluebells at Lissadell.

Clouds lift over Ben Bulben.
Other children run across
the great lawns
and through the house,
their cries echo
an earlier splendour.

The light. The weather. Now.

Ten Haiku

Rain

How still the garden
after rain –
in the gauze of evening
moths shine.

Flag Iris

The cuckoo's singing
at dawn –
and yellow flag iris
open to the sky.

Wind

So loud the wind –
my windows pelted
with wet leaves –
hiss of the kettle.

Moon

I call the old man back
as the moon rolls
in the sky – wild duck
cry out.

Ivory

A wedding gift,
the ivory-handled knives –
warmed by your fingers.

Lilac

Mist from Knockma
settles on lilac
and shy deer.

Daughter

The path takes her
through a dark forest —
the planter's daughter.

Silver Birch

Silver birch grown
tall, near fields
and hills in summer —
the heart breaks.

Blossoms

Two woodpigeons
on an apple bough —
white blossoms
rain.

Night

The night, the night —
not always deep
but lost as seashells
in surf.

Chrysanthemums in November

Looking is not enough. Learn.
Take hedgerows clad in frost, stiff tapestries.
Wild duck rise from the lake,
are lost in the trees.

Bracken rots in fields, bare willows
tremble between earth and sky.
Listen. There is music in the alders,
notes shift with the wind.

Your voice calls out. Hesitantly
you bring me chrysanthemums.
I carry them into the room. Winter
is suddenly coloured red, gold, ivory.

Bringing Bread

This is the day
the saddest month turns.
Sun floods through big windows.
Outside the stones are wet
and a wind howls.

Trees sway over the wall.
One crow swings
on a telephone wire.
I carry bread and water
to the feeding station.

Then they gather: robin,
blackbird, linnet,
finch, woodpigeon.

Instead of reading old letters
or dreaming in dregs of tea-leaves,
I have chosen this small act.
In return I receive
a garden filled with birds,
a sky where clouds
break, letting in such light.

Five Poems in Spring

Again
the cherry buds
burst through.

White swans
swim
to the shore
beyond.

So many
camellias
live.

Under
one umbrella
love sighs.

Spring
and one
snowdrop
in dark earth.

The Broken Fanlight

in memory of my mother

Willows, meadowsweet
and haycocks in July
shimmer in the heat
under storm clouds and sky.

Standing still, I hear
a cricket in the ditch,
hack hack its unmistakeable
sound, rich in its own way.

I remember all
I had to say
that time I saw you,
in the blue coat I sent

from where our story began;
tucked in its folds and pockets,
sad letters, black on white paper,

the fanlight over the door
of the house you left,

broken, like all the heart must accept.

The Light on Muckish – Two Poems

in memory of James Simmons (1933 - 2001)

October rain and wind
tear the arum lilies.
Atlantic salt wilts late roses,
creeps under willow leaves.

You see nothing of storms
that lash the beach
or waves that pound
upwards onto rocks.

It is light and shadow on Muckish
you watch from a window
framing wife and child
who wave to you from rowans.

The Colour of Opals

Between Dunfanaghy and Gortahork
you found Falcarragh
and a house
for family, poetry, song.

Calling your wife to see
morning light
you dreamed
of all you wished to rescue
from your life.

Yet all changed
when illness laid
her hand on you.

You know the sound
wind makes when it howls
in Donegal. Earth turns,
growth is stunted.

Look at the seabirds
fly inland towards Errigal,
their wings
the colour of opals.

To the Light Beyond

Spring light. Dark
long covered you.
Stones barred the way.
Through cracks you see
into the forest,
deeper than you expected.

So long you waited for air
to move lightly around you,
for the heart lift.

From where you are,
trees, buildings
under the sky
are still. You know
brightness that travels well,
crossing over
the ordinary. Beyond.

Shadows

In winter from dark to light
I celebrate. Candles in cut glass
throw shadows over the room.
The souls of the dead know
what they know as they talk
into the night and leave
imprints of their feet on the stairs.

Archway and Field of Light

Only the archway is dark.
Who knows what is concealed
in the courtyard beyond?
Doors and windows either side
reveal nothing; yet sunlight
is reflected everywhere
and much is possible.

Possible that a woman
bought poppies and sunflowers
this morning in her city,
that her room is filled
with children, the picture
she holds of them, laughing
in a field in France.

Ground Ivy

for Tom MacIntyre

Athair lús, that name
you gave the ground ivy stays.

Leaves cling,
twine, stubbornly hold.

The distance between us grows –
between earth, sky, stone, stream

as I try to draw close
to the nameless, the *doráite*

at the heart of things.

Some Deer

Movement in the trees.
I see standing
and watchful
a herd of deer.

Lime twigs crack underfoot,
the deer take fright
spring one after another
deep into the woods.

Next day four appear
and I meet their gaze.
They stand still,
a grey rain on their pelts.

Their oval eyes
look on pines and oaks,
on the earth,
on the chasm of starry night.

In a dream that night
they are mirrored
in a window-pane
as an army goes by.

Reflected in the knife
I use to cut bread
are the deer
who quiet the heart.

Swan

Better I had not seen you
with your webbed feet
on the street
where I grew up.

On a clear January day
you left the Garavogue.
What did you seek?

Better to swim
on the still water, hold
your own counsel
or make love to your mate.

Ben Bulben's shadow
moves closer to town.

You have no song.
What use your inarticulate
wishes? Mine are old
and it is of death
you remind me.

I bring spring flowers
to my parents' grave
in the old cemetery, Sligo.
The light fades fast
and someone plays
a tin whistle in the street.

I sing my own song.

III

The Street of Sighs – La Colonia, Uruguay

But I have loved this earth
because I have not seen another.

Osip Mandelstam

So, once more I see old women
whisper together at their doors.
I turn because I am not one of them.

I watch the sunlight whiten
cobblestones, houses, closed windows
on the Street of Sighs

and take my first step here,
then a second, a third,
never forgetting the shelter of mountains

over the disappeared, their vague traces.

Again the Street of Sighs

My soul and yours
are alone in this street.

It is quiet, ordinary,
nothing seems to happen.

My journey was long
before I found myself here.

I crossed and re-crossed
oceans, continents, mountains.

This street comforts me
for it holds a promise

that despite my sigh,
the heartbreak I hide,

I am an observer
of the life it sees,

made sometimes invisible, but
in the end eternal, in moving light.

The Sea Pinks at Isla Negra

in memory of Pablo Neruda (1904 - 1973)

In your final days at Isla Negra,
barely able to hold a pen, you watched
the Pacific surge on the rocks below.

Brought to you by the ocean, your writing table
faced the window. Your wife, Mathilde,
told the story of its coming.

"Mathilde," you said one day, "come,
something is being carried to me
by the sea." All day you waited

on the shore, all day the object
came nearer and nearer.
At sunset it found safe harbour

untouched by rocks or elements. Mathilde
helped carry it indoors – the lid
of a sea-chest – the ocean's gift.

On this your final verses were written.
When you and Mathilde were gone
someone planted sea pinks on your grave,

little ministers of hope and love.
Here too, engraved in black granite,
are your two names side by side.

Red Cloud, Nebraska

The history of every country begins in the heart
of a man or a woman.

Willa Cather, *O Pioneers!*

That you had brought me this far
from my country of rain,
to prairies and desolation
was in itself enough.

I walked the wide street
of Red Cloud. She walked there too,
leaned against her beloved trees,
oak and silver-breasted birches,
and saw in the hearts of men and women
everything make-believe and real.

Silence of the Sleeping Birds

after Jorge Luis Borges

I never thought of birds like that
until I read your poem,
'The South'.
Entering sleep, the absence
of birdsong seemed natural,
even necessary.

On this bright and light-filled
winter morning, the garden is alive
with the music of linnet and thrush,
scent of winter jasmine,
sounds your feet make
on icy ground
as you walk towards the feeder.

And so, I had slept under
the ancient stars,
in silence.

Ebertswil, Zürich

Bheir mi ó in the background
and not a whin bush or shivering lamb
on the Alps.

I thought it was the low
stone walls, the Atlantic's whistling
that I missed.

But one seashell to hold close
to my ear would do,
and rain on my face.

Notes and Dedications

Ground Ivy
athair lús is Irish for the title of this poem. *Doráite* in Irish means "the unutterable."

Ebertswil, Zürich
Bheir mi ó is the title of an old Irish love song / lament, well known in the public domain of Irish and Scottish traditional airs.

Heather Island
The title of this collection is taken from the name of an island situated in Tully Lake, Renvyle, Connemara, County Galway, still owned by descendents of Oliver St. John Gogarty (1878 – 1957).

Isla Negra
One of three homes owned by Pablo Neruda in Chile and the one in which he died in 1973.

The author wishes to dedicate some of the poems included in this collection to Mark Granier, Nuala Ní Dhomhnaill, Jorie Graham, Eilo Molloy, Richard Murphy and other fellow poets who took part in workshops at Listowel Writers' Week and the Yeats Summer School over the last number of years.

JOAN MCBREEN is from Sligo. She divides her time between Tuam and Renvyle, County Galway. Her poetry collections are: *The Wind Beyond the Wall* (Story Line Press, 1990), *A Walled Garden in Moylough* (Story Line Press and Salmon Poetry, 1995) and *Winter in the Eye – New and Selected Poems* (Salmon Poetry, 2003). She was awarded an MA from University College, Dublin in 1997. Her anthology *The White Page / An Bhileog Bhán – Twentieth-Century Irish Women Poets* was published by Salmon in 1999 and is in its third reprint. Her poetry is published widely in Ireland and abroad and has been broadcast, anthologised and translated into many languages. Her CD *The Long Light on the Land – Selected Poems*, read to a background of traditional Irish airs and classical music, was produced by Ernest Lyons Productions, Castlebar, County Mayo in 2004. She has given readings and talks in many universities in the USA including Emory, Villanova, De Paul (Chicago), Cleveland, Lenoir Rhynne, N.C. and the University of Missouri-St. Louis.

Joan McBreen's 2009 publications include this collection, *Heather Island* and the anthology *The Watchful Heart – A New Generation of Irish Poets – Poems and Essays*. Together with her ongoing involvement with Irish literary festivals such as the Yeats Summer School, Clifden Arts Week, Listowel Writers' Week and The Cúirt International Festival of Literature, since 2007 she has been Literary Advisor and co-ordinator of the Oliver St. John Gogarty Literary Festival at Renvyle House Hotel, Connemara, Co. Galway.